Praise for F

"Wisdom from the past is the tonic that this little book offers to our Covid-weary society. What Luther's treatise from the sixteenth century lacks in scientific knowledge, it more than makes up for in pragmatic advice for ordering a disordered situation. Kudos to Anna Marie Johnson for bringing this gem to light at this time."

—Rev. Dr. Gordon L. Isaac, Berkshire Professor of Church History and Advent Christian Studies at Gordon-Conwell Theological Seminary

"Put this book into any pocket! Luther is not contemporaneous to us, as the introduction and notes by outstanding expert Anna Marie Johnson show excellently. But his wisdom helps to put a pandemic in its theological place. In respect for God's power, love binds us to our neighbors, who need our hygienic precaution as well as pastoral and health care. Luther guides us to find a prudent way through a pandemic—in the Middle Ages, in our time, and in the time to come."

—Dr. Volker Leppin, Horace Tracy Pitkin Professor of Historical Theology, Yale Divinity School

"Even as our Covid pandemic persists, our need for wisdom in how to deal with it in Christian faith and love only grows. Anna Marie Johnson is to be commended for providing such wisdom. This edition of Luther's ever-timely and ever-poignant 'Whether One May Flee from a Deadly Plague' is a gift from the Reformation past to the present."

—Dr. Ronald K. Rittgers, chair in Lutheran studies and professor of the history of Christianity, Duke Divinity School

"Reading Luther has never been more applicable. With five hundred years of distance, he gives timeless advice about handling epidemics with 'love of neighbor as guiding principle.' A popular and widespread pamphlet in its own time, which ought to be read again today. The edition is carefully introduced and annotated by Anna Marie Johnson."

—Dr. Anna Vind, associate professor, Section of Church History, Faculty of Theology, University of Copenhagen

FLEEING PLAGUE

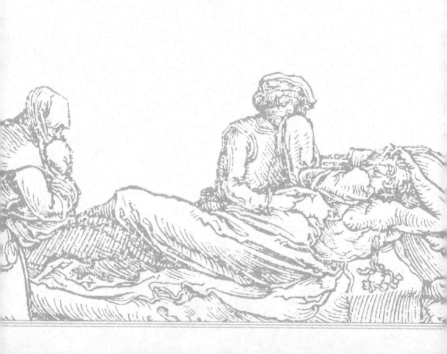

FLEEING PLAGUE

Medieval Wisdom for a Modern Health Crisis

Based on
Martin Luther's
"Whether One May Flee from a Deadly Plague" (1527)

Introduction and Annotations by
Anna Marie Johnson

Fortress Press
Minneapolis

Contents

Abbreviations

BC   *The Book of Concord: The Confessions of the Evangelical Lutheran Church.* Robert Kolb and Timothy J. Wengert, eds. Charles Arand, Eric Gritsch, Robert Kolb, William Russell, James Schaaf, Jane Strohl, Timothy J. Wengert, trans. (Minneapolis: Fortress, 2000).

Brecht   Martin Brecht, *Martin Luther*, trans. James L. Schaff, 3 vols. (Philadelphia and Minneapolis: Fortress Press, 1985–1993).

LW   *Luther's Works, American edition.* 55 vols. (Philadelphia: Fortress; St. Louis: Concordia, 1955–1986).

VD   Verzeichnis der im deutschen Sprachbereich erschienenen Drucke des XVI. Jahrhunderts. 25 vols. (Stuttgart: Hiersemann, 1983–2000).

WA   Luther, Martin. *Luthers Werke: Kritische Gesamtausgabe. [Schriften.]* 73 vols. (Weimar: H. Böhlau 1883–2009).

WA Br   Luther, Martin. *Luthers Werke: Kritische Gesamtausgabe: Briefwechsel,* 12 vols. (Weimar: H. Böhlau, 1930–1985).

WA TR   Luther, Martin. *Luthers Werke: Kritische Gesamtausgabe. Tischreden.* 6 vols. (Weimar: H. Böhlau, 1912–1921).

Preface

I have loved this treatise by Luther since the first time I encountered it. It encapsulates the best of Luther in so many ways: his call to vigorous faith, his compassion toward those who cannot summon that faith, his concrete recommendations for dealing with temptation, his firm insistence on caring for one's neighbor, and his equally firm insistence that Christians not be foolhardy or showy. My appreciation for *Whether One May Flee from a Deadly Plague* only grew during the Covid-19 pandemic, when Luther's keen insights and wise advice resonated with me even more than I expected, helping to orient my faith to the realities of a very disorienting time.

I was not alone in this increased appreciation. Despite the span of almost 500 years between Luther's advice and the Covid-19 pandemic, this work was read and hailed by many in the midst of the twenty-first-century pandemic. The magazine *Christianity Today* published it in full on its website in May 2020, in addition to several other articles that mined the treatise for modern guidance. In the first weeks of the pandemic, *The Hill*, a website dedicated to politics and public policy, ran an opinion piece called "The plague, coronavirus, and Martin Luther—and why they all matter now," which outlined Luther's take on the responsibilities of various community members and recommended his advice in its entirety for the modern situation. A November 2020 article in *Religion News Service* noted the attention Luther's letter was receiving and touted it as a guide to Christian ethics in the twenty-first-century pandemic.[a]

In perhaps the real test of relevance in current media culture, this treatise also inspired multiple memes and quotations on social media during the pandemic. One was posted on the official Facebook page of the Evangelical Lutheran Church in America with the caption, "We pray AND we act."

---

a   Emily McFarlan Miller, "Luther's Pandemic Advice Goes Viral – 500 Years Later." https://religionnews.com/2020/11/20/what-would-luther-do-protestant-reformers-pandemic-advice-goes-viral-500-years-later/

I shall ask God mercifully to protect us.

Then I shall fumigate, help purify the air, administer medicine, and take it.

I shall avoid places and persons where my presence is not needed in order not to become contaminated and thus perchance infect and pollute others.

- Martin Luther, 1527

Posted on ELCA Facebook page, August 4, 2020 with the caption: "We pray AND we act. 16th century counsel from Martin Luther's *Whether One May Flee from a Deadly Plague*."

The treatise was even subject to misinterpretation and controversy, so much so that the fact-checking website, Snopes, ran an explainer on what Luther really said.[b] Apparently some online sources had taken out of context his statement that, if his help was needed, he "would not avoid person or place," using this quote to claim that Luther was against taking precautions because he

b   https://www.snopes.com/fact-check/martin-luther-plague-quote/

trusted God to protect him. Snopes and other online commentators countered with other quotes from this treatise, showing how he both discouraged excessive fear and urged Christians to take preventative measures to protect themselves and others.

The treatise is also a reminder that the Covid-19 pandemic is anything but "unprecedented," as news outlets have often described it. This pandemic is unprecedented for most of us, but only because we have been quite fortunate. Pandemics have happened regularly throughout the course of human history, and, like the early modern bubonic plague, many of them were much worse than Covid. Even today, many parts of the world experience regular epidemics; yellow fever, dengue fever, and sleeping sickness are common occurrences for millions of people. Much of humanity constantly lives with the uncertainty that most modern Westerners are experiencing for the first time.

One of the consolations that history offers is the recognition that many people before us have undergone massive challenges and tragedies. Our ancestors also endured pandemics and other disasters, most of them with far fewer resources than we have. The historical documents they left behind gift us with this perspective, help us summon courage and faith, and remind us that, pandemic or no pandemic, love of God and neighbor are the heart of Christian life. In a world in which ideas and advice are often outdated by the next news cycle, I hope you enjoy reading Luther's advice to his contemporaries. May it strengthen your faith, lead you to hope, and move you to love God and your neighbor amid our own generation's trials.

Introduction

The bubonic plague in western Europe began in the mid-fourteenth century and recurred in cycles through the end of the seventeenth century. Its spread was swift and its toll devastating. The plague entered through Italian and French shipping ports in 1347. By 1349 it had reached Germany, and by 1351 it had spread to nearly all of Europe. The initial outbreak abated in 1353, but the disease reappeared in five- to twelve-year cycles throughout the fourteenth century, and in longer intervals thereafter.

There is some question about the biological cause of the disease, but most historians and epidemiologists think that the early modern plague was caused by the bacillus *Yersinia pestis*, a pathogen first identified in 1918.[a] This bacillus is transmitted via fleas who feed on infected

a   The most thorough argument against this thesis is Samuel K. Cohen Jr.'s *The Black Death Transformed: Disease and Culture in Early Renaissance Europe* (London: Arnold Publishers, 2002).

rats, then bite humans. The increase in trade in the four-teenth century meant that infected rats and fleas were able to spread the disease quickly. The Black Death, as this mid-fourteenth-century epidemic is known, came on the heels of several famines during the late thirteenth and early fourteenth centuries, which had already taken their toll on society. In the words of historian Edward Peters, the plague "struck a population weakened by hunger and lack of resistance, crowded into cities, more mobile than in any period of Europe's history since the fifth and sixth centuries, and thus extremely vulnerable to contagion—a principle it did not understand."[b]

By the end of the initial 1347–1351 epidemic, approximately one-third of Europe's population

Allegory of Demon of the Plague, engraved illustration from *Feldtbuch der Wundarzney* (*Fieldbook of Wound Surgery*) by Hans von Gersdorff (Strasburg, 1540)

b   Edward Peters, *Europe and the Middle Ages*, 3d ed. (Upper Saddle River, NJ: Prentice-Hall, 1997), 332.

had died.[c] Repeated bouts of plague continued to take their toll, and the population did not begin to recover until the late fifteenth century as the epidemic slowed. Even those who survived an infection of the plague were weakened, and thus vulnerable to other diseases. In addition, the plague disrupted the goods and services that sustained health, making life more difficult for survivors. The regional nature of the epidemic meant that some towns and areas were spared entirely, while others were hit hard and even deserted. Estimates on overall fatality rates for the plague have ranged widely, from 30 percent to 60 percent. The German title for this work illustrates the virulence associated with the disease: the English translations have typically called this work "Whether One May Flee from a Deadly Plague," but the original title given to it, probably by the printer, was simply, "Whether One May Flee Death."[d]

---

c   Jan de Vries, "Population," in Thomas A. Brady Jr., Heiko A. Oberman, and James D. Tracy, eds., *Handbook of European History, 1400–1600: Late Middle Ages, Renaissance and Reformation*, vol. 1: *Structures and Assertions* (Leiden: Brill, 1994).

d   Luther's handwritten manuscript of this work has "OB MAN FVR DEM STERBEN FLIEHEN SOLL" written across the top, although not in Luther's hand (WA 23:338).

INTRODUCTION

The plague could take three forms in humans. In its bubonic form, the lymph nodes near the flea bite would become extremely large, forming the "bubo" that gave this form of plague one of its names. (The other name, "Black Death," comes from the necrotic black plaques that often formed on the skin.) From the lymph nodes, the infection might then travel to the central nervous system, causing high fever, headache, disorientation, and finally death. Sometimes, however, the infection would enter the bloodstream directly, causing the septicemic (blood-borne) form of the disease, a highly fatal form. Another highly fatal form of the plague was pneumonic plague, in which the disease entered the lungs. The pneumonic form was particularly dangerous because it could be spread to others by cough, bypassing the lymphatic system and entering directly into the lungs. When this happened, the fatality rate was nearly 100 percent.[e] The sudden onset and high mortality of the disease fostered an acute concern with the issue of salvation among both theologians and laypeople. One outgrowth of this piqued interest was the appearance of books that advised people what they should do on the deathbed

---

e   Ann Carmichael, "Bubonic Plague," in Kenneth F. Kiple, ed., *The Cambridge World History of Human Disease* (Cambridge: Cambridge University Press, 1993), 629–30.

to die a good, Christian death, a genre to which Luther also contributed.[f]

Luther's treatise on whether one may flee when plague strikes was prompted by a request from the clergy of Breslau, a city in Silesia. They wondered whether a Christian could flee home and labors on account of the plague, and they asked the Silesian reformer Johann Hess (1490–1547) to solicit Luther's opinion. Luther did not respond at first, possibly because a health scare on 6 July 1527 had left him with headaches that impeded his reading and writing. Hess repeated the request for counsel at least once, and Luther began his response in late July.[1]*

It is very possible that Luther was motivated to write on the topic by rumors that the plague was raging near Wittenberg. Indeed, it reached Wittenberg on 2 August 1527. Within weeks part of the university was moved to Jena. Luther's prince wanted Luther to go to Jena as well, but he refused because he felt he was needed in Wittenberg to minister to the sick and dying. He was also inclined to stay in Wittenberg because he had been experiencing health problems and spiritual trials since April of that year, and he found that the intercessions

---

f   See his *Sermon on Preparing for Death* (LW 32: 99–115; *The Annotated Luther* 4: 283–305).

*   Numbered annotations can be found at the back of the book.

of his friends in Wittenberg gave him some relief from those trials.[g] The arrival of the plague, as well as Luther's ill health, seems to have interrupted his writing at least twice; Luther's handwritten manuscript shows two distinct shifts in the type of paper he used and in his handwriting. The work was finally completed in either October or November, and the plague in Wittenberg ended in the last part of November.

Luther's response was thoroughly pragmatic. It focused on Christians' responsibility to care for the sick and to use the means that God gives to limit the plague's destruction. He lauded those who can face the plague without fear of death, but he emphasized that those with "weak faith" can flee in good conscience as long as they are not needed to care for someone or to maintain a public service. To be sure, the question of whether to flee was a question entertained only by a certain class: those who had somewhere to go and who could afford to suspend their livelihoods. The plague hit the poor harder than the affluent because of their limited ability to flee, their crowded and often rat-infested housing, and their

---

g   Martin Brecht, *Martin Luther: Shaping and Defining the Reformation 1521–1532*, trans. James L. Schaaf (Minneapolis: Fortress Press, 1990), 207, 209 (hereafter Brecht 2).

inferior nutrition.[h] Luther's response to the question of fleeing called on those who were able to flee to suspend that privilege if their vocations (either professional or within the household) meant that they were responsible for the well-being of others.

Luther used the opportunity of this open letter to address other plague-related circumstances as well. He encouraged municipalities to create hospitals so that care of the sick was dependable. He urged cities to move graveyards outside of the city so that they would be peaceful places of respect and contemplation. He also addressed extreme pieties that had sprung up in response to the plague. Some argued that Christians should ignore plague precautions because the plague is God's will, and God could heal people through super-natural means. Luther responded that God has given doctors and medicines that ought to be used to ensure that one does not sacrifice one's own life or, much worse, the lives of many others. In all matters related to the

---

h   For more on the plague and poverty, see Ann G. Carmichael, *Plague and the Poor in Renaissance Florence* (Cambridge: Cambridge University Press, 1986); Paul Stark, *The Impact of the Plague in Tudor and Stuart England* (London: Routledge, 1985); and A. Lloyd Moote and Dorothy C. Moote, *The Great Plague: The Story of London's Most Deadly Year* (Baltimore: Johns Hopkins University Press, 2004), esp. 75–94.

plague, love of neighbor was the guiding principle, and that love was manifested best in the faithful and often grueling care for the sick.

It is worth noting that Luther lived up to the advice he gave. Far from fleeing, the Luther household took in several people who were infected with the plague. His son and only child at that point, Hans, also became infected but survived. Luther's wife was pregnant with their second child, and Luther worried about both mother and child. The baby, Elizabeth, was born sickly on 10 December, and died just shy of eight months old, quite possibly because of her mother's exposure to the plague during pregnancy.[i] During this time, he spoke often of his spiritual trials and physical ailments, which he attributed to the devil. Ironically, his endurance of those trials seemed to strengthen his fortitude during the plague because he considered the attacks of the devil to be much more fearsome than the plague.

Luther's advice apparently struck a chord with a plague-weary public. This letter was reprinted at least ten times within 1527,[j] and seventeen additional times

---

i   Brecht 2:204.

j   VD 16 L 5513–23.

later in the sixteenth century.[k] Its popularity ebbed and flowed in the second half of the sixteenth century as the plague came and went. It was printed at least five times in the seventeenth century, as the plague continued to preoccupy western Europe.[l]

---

k   VD 16 L 5524–37; ZV 10175; ZV 18113; ZV 22088.

l   VD 17 1:680482L; 1:680496X; 3:315927D; 14:018701R; 14:668013D.

This painting by Josse Lieferinxe (c. 1497) is called *Saint Sebastian Interceding for the Plague Stricken*. St. Sebastian was one of the main saints thought to protect and aid those affected by the plague. Sebastian was martyred around 300 CE with arrows. In this painting, St. Sebastian pleads before God on behalf of the plague victims seen below while a demon and an angel prepare to fight. The scene on the ground shows several deceased plague victims wrapped in shrouds and a still-living plague victim lying on the ground. Note the swollen lymph gland, or bubo, on the living victim's neck.

Title page of *Whether One May Flee from a Deadly Plague* (1527)

Whether One May Flee from a Deadly Plague[2]

To the Reverend Doctor Johann Hess, pastor at Breslau, and to his fellow-servants of the gospel of Jesus Christ

Martinus Luther

[Luther's Introduction][a]

Grace and peace from God our Father and our Lord Jesus Christ. Your letter, sent to us at Wittenberg, was received some time ago. You wish to know whether it is proper for a Christian to run away from a deadly plague. I should

---

a   Headings in brackets have been added to the original text to aid in reading.

have answered long ago, but God has for some time disciplined and scourged me so severely that I have been unable to do much reading or writing.[3] Furthermore, it occurred to me that God, our merciful Father, has endowed you so richly with wisdom and truth in Christ that you yourself should be well qualified to decide this matter or even weightier problems in his spirit and grace without our assistance.

But now you keep on writing to me and have, so to speak, humbled yourself in requesting our view on this matter so that, as St. Paul repeatedly teaches, we may always agree with one another and be of one mind [1 Cor. 1:10; 2 Cor. 13:11; Phil. 2:2]. Therefore we here give you our opinion as far as God grants us to understand and perceive. This we would humbly submit to your judgment and to that of all devout Christians for them to come to their own decision and conclusion, as is proper. Since the rumor of death is to be heard in these and many other parts also,[4] we have permitted these instructions of ours to be printed because others might also want to make use of them.

To begin with, some people are of the firm opinion that one need not and should not run away from a deadly plague. Rather, since death is God's punishment, which he sends upon us for our sins, we must submit

Two wings of a plague altarpiece from the Augustinian Monastery zu den Wengen in Ulm by artist Martin Schaffner (1478–1546). In the scene an angry God the Father punishes the sinful with plague arrows. The sufferers send their prayers to God through the mediation of two plague saints, Roch and Sebastian, who pass their pleas to Mary (lower left). Mary, in turn, presents the prayers to her son Jesus, who, showing his wounds, presents the prayers to his father, God.

to God and with a true and firm faith patiently await our punishment.[5] They look upon running away as an outright wrong and as lack of belief in God. Others take the position that one may properly flee, particularly if one holds no public office.

I cannot censure the former for their excellent decision. They uphold a good cause, namely, a strong faith in God, and deserve commendation because they desire every Christian to hold to a strong, firm faith. It takes more than a milk faith[6] to await a death before which most of the saints themselves have been and still are in dread. Who would not acclaim these earnest people to whom death is a little thing? They willingly accept God's chastisement, doing so without tempting God, as we shall hear later on.

Since it is generally true of Christians that few are strong and many are weak, one simply cannot place the same burden upon everyone.[7] A person who has a strong faith can drink poison and suffer no harm, Mark 16[:18], while one who has a weak faith would thereby suffer death. Peter could walk upon the water because he was strong in faith. When he began to doubt and his faith weakened, he sank and almost drowned. When those who are strong travel with those who are weak, the strong must try not to walk at a pace based on their strength lest they walk their weak companions nearly to death.[b] Christ does not want his weak ones to be abandoned, as St. Paul teaches in Rom. 15[:1] and 1 Cor. 12[:22ff.].

To put it briefly and concisely, running away from death may happen in one of two ways. First, it may happen in disobedience to God's word and command, for instance, in the case of those who are imprisoned for the sake of God's word and who, to escape death, deny and repudiate God's word.[8] In such a situation everyone has Christ's plain mandate and command not to flee but rather to suffer death, as he says, "Whoever denies me before men, I will also deny before my Father who is in heaven" and "Do not fear those who kill the body but cannot kill the soul," Matt. 10[:28, 33].

[Who Must Normally Stay, and under What Conditions They Might Leave]

Those who are engaged in a spiritual ministry such as preachers and pastors must likewise remain steadfast before the peril of death. We have a plain command from Christ, "A good shepherd lays down his life for the sheep

---

b   Here and at some other points in the text, Luther's singular pronouns have been replaced with plural pronouns to avoid the use of generic masculine pronouns.

but the hireling sees the wolf coming and flees" [John 10:11].[9] For when people are dying, they most need a spiritual ministry which strengthens and comforts their consciences by word and sacrament and in faith overcomes death.[10] However, where enough preachers are available in one locality and they agree to encourage the other clergy to leave in order not to expose themselves needlessly to danger, I do not consider such conduct sinful because spiritual services are provided and because they would have been ready and willing to stay if it had been necessary. We read that St. Athanasius fled from his church that his life might be spared because many others were there to administer his office.[11] Similarly, the brethren in Damascus lowered Paul in a basket over the wall to make it possible for him to escape, Acts 9[:25].[c] And also in Acts 19[:30] Paul allowed himself to be kept from risking danger in the marketplace because it was not essential for him to do so.[12]

Accordingly, all those in public office such as mayors, judges, and the like are under the obligation to remain. This, too, is God's word, which institutes secular authority and commands that town and country be ruled, protected, and preserved, as St. Paul teaches in Rom.

---

c   Paul was being pursued by Jews who were upset by his recent conversion to Christianity.

13[:4], "The governing authorities are God's ministers for your own good." To abandon an entire community that one has been called to govern, to leave it without officials or government, exposed to all kinds of danger such as fires, murder, riots, and every imaginable disaster, is a great sin. It is the kind of disaster the devil would like to instigate wherever there is no law and order. St. Paul says, "Anyone who does not provide for family members denies the faith and is worse than an unbeliever" [1 Tim. 5:8]. On the other hand, if in great weakness they flee but provide capable substitutes to make sure that the community is well governed and protected, as we previously indicated, and if they continually and carefully supervise them [i.e., the substitutes], all that would be proper.

What applies to these two offices [church and state] should also apply to persons who stand in a relationship of service or duty toward one another. A servant should not leave his master nor a maid her mistress except with the knowledge and permission of master or mistress. Again, a master should not desert his servant nor a lady her maid unless suitable provision for their care has been made somewhere. In all these matters it is a divine command that servants and maids should render obedience and by the same token masters and ladies should take care of their servants.[d] Likewise, fathers and mothers are bound by God's law to serve and help their children, and children their fathers and mothers. Likewise, paid public servants such as city physicians, city clerks, and constables, or whatever their titles, should not flee unless they furnish capable substitutes who are acceptable to their employer.[13]

In the case of children who are orphaned, guardians or close friends are under obligation either to stay with them or to arrange diligently for other nursing care for their sick friends. Yes, no one should dare leave a neighbor unless there are others who will take care of the sick in their stead and nurse them. In such cases we must respect the word of Christ, "I was sick and you did not visit me . . ." [Matt. 25:41–46]. According to this passage, we are bound to each other in such a way that we should not forsake others in distress. Instead, we are obliged to assist and help them, as we ourselves would like to be helped.

[Who May Flee]

Where no such emergency exists and enough people are available for the care of the sick—whether voluntarily, by duty, or arranged by those who are weak in faith—so

---

d   See Eph. 6:6–9 and Col. 3:33–4:1.

that there is no need for additional helpers, or where the sick do not want them and have refused their services, I judge that they are free either to flee or to remain. If they are sufficiently bold and strong in their faith, let them stay in God's name; that is certainly no sin. If they are weak and fearful, let them flee in God's name as long as they do not neglect their duty toward their neighbors but have made adequate provision for others to provide care. To flee from death and to save one's life is a natural tendency, implanted by God and not forbidden unless it be against God and neighbor,[14] as St. Paul says in Eph. 4 [5:29], "No one ever hates his own flesh, but nourishes and cherishes it." It is even commanded that everyone should as much as possible preserve body and life and not neglect them, as St. Paul says in 1 Cor. 12[:21–26] that God has so ordered the members of the body that each one cares and works for the other.

It is not forbidden but rather commanded that by the sweat of our brow we should seek our daily food, clothing, and all we need, and that we should avoid destruction and disaster whenever we can, as long as we do so without detracting from our love and duty toward our neighbor. How much more appropriate it is therefore to seek to preserve life and avoid death if this can be done without harm to our neighbor, inasmuch as life is more than food and clothing, as Christ himself says in Matt. 5 [6:25].[15] If you are so strong in faith, however, that you can willingly suffer nakedness, hunger, and want without tempting God and without trying to escape, although you could do so, you may continue that way; but do not condemn those who will not or cannot do the same.

Examples in Holy Scripture abundantly prove that to flee from death is not wrong in itself. Abraham was a great saint but he feared death and escaped it by pretending that his wife, Sarah, was his sister.[e] Because he did so without neglecting or adversely affecting his neighbor, it was not counted as a sin against him. His son Isaac did likewise.[f] Jacob also fled from his brother Esau to avoid death at his hands.[g] Likewise, David fled from Saul, and from Absalom.[h] The prophet Uriah escaped from King Jehoiakim and fled into Egypt.[i] The valiant prophet Elijah, 1 Kgs. 19[:3], had destroyed all the

---

e   Gen. 12:10–20; Genesis 20.

f   Gen. 26:6–11.

g   Gen. 27:43–45.

h   1 Sam. 19:10–17; 2 Sam. 15:14.

i   Jer. 26:21.

prophets of Baal by his great faith, but afterward, when Queen Jezebel threatened him, he became afraid and fled into the desert. Before that, Moses fled into the land of Midian when the king searched for him in Egypt.[j] Many others have done likewise. All of them fled from death when it was possible and saved their lives, yet without depriving their neighbors of anything, but first meeting their obligations toward them.

Yes, you may reply, but these examples do not refer to dying by pestilence but to death under persecution. Answer: Death is death, no matter how it occurs. According to Holy Scripture God sent his four scourges: pestilence, famine, sword, and wild beasts.[k] If it is permissible to flee from one or the other in clear conscience, why not from all four? Our examples demonstrate how the holy fathers escaped from the sword; it is quite evident that Abraham, Isaac, and Jacob fled from the other scourge, namely, hunger and death, when they went to Egypt to escape famine, as we are told in Genesis [40–47]. Likewise, why should one not run away from wild beasts? I hear people say, "If war or the Turks come, we should not flee from our village or town

---

j   Exod. 2:15.

k   Ezek. 14:21; Rev. 6:1–11.

but stay and await God's punishment by the sword." That is quite true; let those who have a strong faith wait for their death, but they should not condemn those who take flight.

Moses flees Egypt (Exod. 2:15)

By such reasoning, when a house is on fire, no one should run outside or rush to help because such a fire is also a punishment from God.[16] Those who fall into deep water dare not save themselves by swimming but instead must surrender to the water as to a divine punishment. Very well, do so if you can but do not tempt

God, and allow others to do as much as they are capable of doing. Likewise, if someone breaks a leg, is wounded or bitten, he should not seek medical aid but say, "It is God's punishment. I shall bear it until it heals by itself." Freezing weather and winter are also God's punishment and can cause death. Why run to get inside or near a fire? Be strong and stay outside until it becomes warm again. We should then need no apothecaries or drugs or physicians because all illnesses are punishment from God. Hunger and thirst are also great punishments and torture. Why do you eat and drink instead of letting yourself be punished until hunger and thirst stop of themselves? Ultimately, such talk will lead to the point where we abbreviate the Lord's Prayer and no longer pray, "deliver us from evil, Amen," since we would have to stop praying to be saved from hell and stop seeking to escape it. It, too, is God's punishment as is every kind of evil. Where would all this end?

From what has been said we derive this guidance: We must pray against every form of evil and guard against it to the best of our ability in order not to act contrary to God, as was previously explained. If it be God's will that evil come upon us and destroy us, none of our precautions will help us. We must all take this to heart: first of all, if we feel bound to remain where death rages in order to serve our neighbor, let us commend ourselves to God and say, "Lord, I am in your hands; you have kept me here; your will be done. I am your lowly creature. You can kill me or preserve me in this pestilence in the same way as if I were in fire, water, drought, or any other danger." If we are free, however, and can escape, let us commend ourselves and say, "Lord God, I am weak and fearful. Therefore I am running away from evil and am doing what I can to protect myself against it. I am nevertheless in your hands in this danger as in any other which might overtake me. Your will be done. My flight alone will not succeed of itself because calamity and harm are everywhere. Moreover, the devil never sleeps. He is a murderer from the beginning [John 8:44] and tries everywhere to instigate murder and misfortune."[17]

[Love of Neighbor in All Circumstances[18]]

In the same way we must accord our neighbors[19] the same treatment in other troubles and perils also, and we owe it to our neighbors to do so. If our neighbors' house is on fire, love compels me to run to help them extinguish the flames. If there are enough other people around to put the fire out, I may either go home or remain to help. If someone falls into the water or into a pit I dare not turn away but must hurry to help the person as best I can. If there are others to do it, I am released from this responsibility. If I see that someone is hungry or thirsty, I cannot ignore that person but must offer food and drink, not considering whether I would risk impoverishing myself by doing so. Those who will not help or support others unless they can do so without affecting their safety or property will never help their neighbor. They will always reckon with the possibility that doing so will bring some disadvantage and damage, danger and loss. No neighbor can live alongside another without risk to one's own safety, property, wife, or child. We must run the risk that fire or some other accident will start in our neighbor's house and destroy us bodily or deprive us of our goods, spouse, children, and all we have.

Those who do not do that for their neighbors, but instead forsake them and leave them to their misfortune, become murderers in the sight of God, as St. John states in his epistles, "All who hate a brother or sister are murderers," and again, "How does God's love abide in anyone who has the world's goods and sees a brother or sister in need and yet refuses to help?" [1 John 3:15, 17]. That is also one of the sins which God attributed to the city of Sodom when he speaks through the prophet Ezekiel [16:49], "Behold, this was the guilt of your sister

Sodom: she and her daughters had pride, excess of food, and prosperous ease, but did not aid the poor and needy." Christ, therefore, will condemn them as murderers on the Last Day when he will say, "I was sick and you did not visit me" [Matt. 25:43]. If that shall be the judgment upon those who have failed to visit the sick and needy or to offer them relief, what will become of those who abandoned them and let them lie there like dogs and pigs? Yes, how will they fare who rob the poor of the little they have and plague them in all kinds of ways?[20] That is what the tyrants do to the poor who accept the gospel. But let that be; they have their condemnation.

[Recommendations for Communities]

It would be well, where there is an efficient government in cities and states, to maintain municipal homes and hospitals staffed with people to take care of the sick so that patients from private homes can be sent there—as was the intent and purpose of our forefathers with so many pious bequests, hospices, hospitals, and infirmaries—so that it should not be necessary for every citizen to maintain a hospital in each home.[21] That would indeed be a fine, commendable, and Christian arrangement to which everyone should offer generous help and contributions, particularly the government. Where there are no such institutions—and they exist in only a few places—we must give hospital care and be nurses for one another in any extremity or risk the loss of salvation and the grace of God. Thus it is written in God's word and command, "Love your neighbor as yourself," and in Matt. 7[:12], "So whatever you wish that [others] would do to you, do so to them."

Now if a deadly epidemic strikes, we should stay where we are, make our preparations, and take courage in the fact that we are mutually bound together (as previously indicated) so that we cannot desert one another or flee from one another. First, we can be sure that God's punishment has come upon us, not only to chastise us for our sins but also to test our faith and love—our faith in that we may see and experience how we should act toward God; our love in that we may recognize how we should act toward our neighbor. I am of the opinion that all the epidemics, like any plague, are spread among the people by evil spirits who poison the air or exhale a pestilential breath, which puts a deadly poison into the flesh.[22] Nevertheless, this is God's decree and punishment to which we must patiently submit and serve our neighbor, risking our lives in this manner as St. John teaches, "If Christ laid down his life for us, we ought to lay down our lives for our brothers and sisters" [1 John 3:16].

[Fighting the Devil by Loving the Neighbor]

When anyone is overcome by horror and repugnance in the presence of a sick person we should take courage and strength in the firm assurance that it is the devil who stirs up such abhorrence, fear, and loathing in our hearts. He is such a bitter, knavish devil that he not only unceasingly tries to slay and kill us, but also takes delight in making us deathly afraid, worried, and apprehensive so that we should regard dying as horrible and have no rest or peace all through our life. And so the devil would excrete us out of this life[23] as he tries to make us despair of God and become unwilling and unprepared to die. Then, under the stormy and dark sky of fear and anxiety, he makes us forget and lose Christ, our light and life, and desert our neighbors in their troubles. We would sin thereby against God and humanity; that would be the devil's glory and delight. Because we know that the devil's game is to induce such fear and dread, we should instead minimize it, take courage just to spite and annoy him, and send those terrors right back to him. And we should arm ourselves with this answer to the devil:[24]

"Get away, you devil, with your terrors! Just because you hate it, I'll spite you by going the more quickly to help my sick neighbor. I'll pay no attention to you. I've got two heavy blows to use against you: the first one is that I know that helping my neighbor is a deed well-pleasing to God and all the angels; by this deed I do God's will and render true service and obedience to him. Especially if you hate it so and are so strongly opposed to it, it must be particularly acceptable to God. I'd do this readily and gladly if I could please only one angel who might look with delight on it. But now that it pleases my Lord Jesus Christ and the whole heavenly host because it is the will and command of God, my Father, then how could any fear of you cause me to spoil such joy in heaven or such delight for my Lord? Or how could I, by flattering you, give you and your devils in hell reason to mock and laugh at me? No, you'll not have the last word! If Christ shed his blood for me and died for me, why should I not expose myself to some small dangers for his sake and disregard this feeble plague? If you can terrorize, Christ can strengthen me. If you can kill, Christ can give life. If you have poison in your fangs, Christ has far greater medicine. Should not my dear Christ, with his precepts, his kindness, and all his encouragement, be more important in my spirit than you, roguish devil, with your false terrors in my weak flesh? God forbid! Get away, devil. Here is Christ and here am I, his servant in this work. Let Christ prevail! Amen."

The second blow against the devil is God's mighty promise by which he encourages those who minister to the needy. He says in Ps. 41[:1–3], "Blessed are those who consider the poor. The Lord will deliver them in the day of trouble. The Lord will protect them and keep them alive; the Lord will bless them on earth and not give them up to the will of their enemies. The Lord will sustain them on their sickbed. In their illness he will heal all their infirmities." Are not these glorious and mighty promises of God heaped up upon those who minister to the needy? What should terrorize us or frighten us away from such great and divine comfort? The service we can render to the needy is indeed such a small thing in comparison with God's promises and rewards that St. Paul says to Timothy, "Godliness is of value in every way, and it holds promise both for the present life and for the life to come" [1 Tim. 4:8]. Godliness is nothing else but service to God. Service to God is indeed service to our neighbor. It is proved by experience that those who nurse the sick with love, devotion, and sincerity are generally protected. Though they are poisoned, they are not harmed. As the psalm says, "in his illness you heal all his infirmities" [Ps. 41:3], that is, you change his bed of sickness into a bed of health. A person who attends a patient because of greed, or with the expectation of an inheritance or some personal advantage in such services, should not be surprised if eventually he is infected, disfigured, or even dies before he comes into possession of that estate or inheritance.[25]

But those who serve the sick for the sake of God's gracious promise (though they may accept a suitable payment, to which they are entitled inasmuch as every laborer deserves a wage) will have the great assurance that they shall also be cared for. God himself shall be their attendant and their physician, too. What an attendant he is! What a physician! Friend, what are all the physicians, apothecaries, and attendants in comparison to God? Should that not encourage us to go and serve the sick, even though they might have as many contagious boils on them as they have hairs on their bodies, and though we might be bent double carrying a hundred plague-ridden bodies! What do all kinds of pestilence or devils mean over against God, who binds and obliges himself to be our attendant and physician? Shame and more shame on you, you out-and-out unbeliever, for despising such great comfort and letting yourself become more frightened by some small boil or some uncertain danger than emboldened by such sure and faithful promises of God! What would it avail you if all physicians and the entire world were at your service, but God were not present? Again, what harm could overtake you if the whole world were to desert you and no physician would remain with you, but God would abide with you with his assurance?[26] Do you not know that you are surrounded as by thousands of angels who watch over you so that you can indeed trample upon the plague, as it is written in Ps. 91[:11–13], "He has given his angels charge of you to guard you in all your ways. On their hands they will bear you up lest you dash your foot against a stone. You will tread upon the lion and the adder, and trample the young lion and the serpent under foot."

Therefore, dear friends, let us not become so desperate as to desert our own whom we are duty-bound to help, and to flee in such a cowardly way in terror of the devil, or to allow him the joy of mocking us and vexing and distressing God and all his angels. For it is certainly true that those who despise such great promises and commands of God and leave their own people destitute violate all of God's laws and are guilty of the murder of the neighbors whom they abandon. I fear that in such a case God's promise will be reversed and changed into horrible threats and the psalm [41] will then read this way against them: "Accursed are those who do not provide for the needy but escape and forsake them. The Lord in turn will not spare them in evil days but will flee from them and desert them. The Lord will not preserve them and keep them alive and will not prosper them on earth but will deliver them into the hands of their enemies. The Lord will not refresh them on their sickbed nor take them from the bed of their illness." For "the measure you give will be the measure you get" [Matt. 7:2]. Nothing else can come of it. It is terrible to hear this, more terrible to be waiting for this to happen, most terrible to experience it. What else can happen if God withdraws his hand and forsakes us except sheer devilment and every kind of evil? It cannot be otherwise if, against God's command, we abandon our neighbor. This fate will surely overtake everyone of this sort, unless they sincerely repent.

This I well know, that if it were Christ or his mother who was laid low by illness, everybody would be so solicitous and would gladly become a servant or helper. Everyone would want to be bold and fearless; nobody would flee but everyone would come running. And yet they don't hear what Christ himself says, "As you did it to one of the least, you did it to me" [Matt. 25:40]. When

DE PEST.

Zonden is Pest.

[*Doch*] *ik zal ze van 't geweld der helle verloſſen,
ik zal ze vry maaken van den dood: ô Dood, waar
zyn uwe peſtilentien? Helle, waar is u verderf? be-
rouw zal van myne oogen verborgen zyn.* Hozea XIII:
vers 14.

Zo

In this etching by Jan Luiken (1649–1712) or his son Casper Luiken (1672–1708), two men lie dying in the foreground of a town square. One of them is given something to drink by a third man, who holds a hand in front of his mouth. Farther away, a dead person is dragged away, people are dying, and bodies are heaped up against a building.

he speaks of the greatest commandment he says, "The second commandment is like [the first commandment], you shall love your neighbor as yourself" [Matt. 22:39]. There you hear that the command to love your neighbor is equal to the greatest commandment to love God, and that what you do or fail to do for your neighbor means doing the same to God. If you wish to serve Christ and to wait on him, very well, you have your sick neighbor close at hand. Go to them and serve them, and you will surely find Christ in them, not outwardly but in his word. If you do not wish or care to serve your neighbor, you can be sure that, if Christ lay there instead, you would not serve him either. You would let him just lie there. It is nothing but an illusion on your part that puffs you up with vain pride, namely, that you would really serve Christ if he were there in person. That is nothing but lies. Those who want to serve Christ in person would surely serve their neighbor as well. This is said as an admonition and encouragement against fear and a disgraceful flight, to which the devil would tempt us, so that we would disregard God's command in our dealings with our neighbor and thus fall into sin on the left hand.[27]

[Those Who Tempt God]

Others sin on the right hand. They are much too rash and reckless, tempting God and disregarding everything which might counteract death and the plague. They disdain the use of medicines; they do not avoid places and persons infected by the plague, but instead light-heartedly make sport of it and wish to prove how independent they are. They say that it is God's punishment; if he wants to protect them he can do so without medicines or our carefulness. This is not trusting God, but rather tempting him. God has created medicines and provided us with intelligence to guard and take good care of the body so that we can live in good health.

If they make no use of intelligence or medicine when they could do so without detriment to their neighbors, such people injure their bodies and must beware lest they become a suicide in God's eyes.[28] By the same reasoning they might forgo eating and drinking, clothing and shelter, and boldly proclaim their faith that if God wanted to preserve them from starvation and cold, he could do so without food and clothing. Actually that would be suicide. It is even more shameful for them to pay no heed to their own bodies and to fail to protect them against the plague the best they are able, and then to infect and poison others who might have remained alive if they had taken care of their bodies as they should have. They are thus responsible before God for their neighbor's death and are a murderer many times over.[29] Indeed, such people behave as though a house were burning in the city and nobody was trying to put the fire out. Instead they give leeway to the flames so that the whole city is consumed, saying that if God so willed, he could save the city without water to quench the fire.

No, my dear friends, that is no good. Use medicine; take potions which can help you; fumigate house, yard, and street;[30] shun persons and places wherever your neighbor does not need your presence or has recovered, and act like someone who wants to help put out the burning city. What else is the epidemic but a fire which instead of consuming wood and straw devours life and body? You ought to think this way: "Very well, by God's decree the enemy has sent us poison and deadly refuse. Therefore I shall ask God mercifully to protect us. Then I shall fumigate, help purify the air, administer medicine, and take it. I shall avoid places and persons where my presence is not needed in order not to become contaminated and thus perchance infect and pollute others, and so cause their death as a result of my negligence. If God should wish to take me, he will surely find me, and I have done what he has expected of me and so I am not responsible for either my own death or the death of others. If my neighbor needs me, however, I shall not avoid place or person but will go freely, as stated above. See, this is such a God-fearing faith because it is neither brash nor foolhardy and does not tempt God.

An apothecary prepares medicinal potions with mortar and pestle.

Moreover, those who have contracted the disease and recovered should keep away from others and not admit others into their presence unless it is necessary.[31] Though they should receive aid in their time of need, as previously pointed out, after their recovery, they should act toward others so that no one becomes unnecessarily endangered on their account and thus they cause another's death. "Whoever loves danger," says the wise man, "will perish by it" [Ecclus. 3:26]. If the people in a city were to show themselves bold in their faith when a neighbor's need so demands, and cautious when no emergency exists, and if everyone would help ward off contagion as best they can, then the death toll would indeed be moderate. But if some are too panicky and desert their neighbors in their plight, and if some are so foolish as not to take precautions but aggravate the contagion, then the devil has a heyday and many will die. On both counts this is a grievous offense to God and to humanity—here it is tempting God; there it is bringing humanity into despair. Then the one who flees, the devil will pursue; the one who stays behind, the devil will hold captive so that no one escapes.

Some are even worse than that. They keep it secret that they have the disease and go among others in the belief that by contaminating and poisoning others they can rid themselves of the plague and so recover. With this idea they enter streets and homes, trying to saddle children or servants with the disease and thus save themselves. I certainly believe that this is the devil's doing, who helps turn the wheel of fate to make this happen. I have been told that some are so incredibly vicious that they circulate among people and enter homes because they are sorry that the plague has not reached that far and wish to carry it in, as though it were a prank, like putting lice into fur garments or flies into someone's living room.[32] I do not know whether I should believe this; if it is true, I do not know whether we Germans are not really devils instead of human beings. It must be admitted that there are some extremely coarse and wicked people. The devil is never idle.

My advice is that if any such persons are discovered, the judge should take them by the ear and turn them over to Master Jack, the hangman, as outright and deliberate murderers.[33] What else are such people but assassins in our town? Here and there an assassin will jab a knife through someone and no one can find the culprit. So these folk infect a child here, a woman there, and can never be caught. They go on laughing as though they had accomplished something. Where this is the case, it would be better to live among wild beasts than with such murderers. I do not know how to preach to such killers.

They pay no heed. I appeal to the authorities to take charge and turn them over to the help and advice not of physicians, but of Master Jack, the hangman.

If in the Old Testament God himself ordered lepers to be banished from the community and compelled to live outside the city to prevent contamination [Leviticus 13–14],[34] we must do the same with this dangerous pestilence so that those who become infected will stay away from other people, or allow themselves to be taken away and given speedy help with medicine. Under such circumstances it is our duty to assist those who are infected and not forsake them in their plight, as I have repeatedly pointed out before. Then the poison is stopped in time, which benefits not only the individual infected but also the whole community, which might be contaminated if one person is permitted to infect others. Our plague here in Wittenberg has been caused by nothing but filth. The air, thank God, is still clean and pure, but some few have been contaminated because of the laziness or recklessness of some. So the devil enjoys himself at the terror and flight which he causes among us. May God thwart him! Amen.

This is what we think and conclude on this subject of fleeing from death by the plague. If you are of a different opinion, may God enlighten you. Amen.

A priest and two assistants carry a pyx containing the elements of Holy Communion to one who is sick. They are standing below a canopy as in a procession. From a 1523 publication of Luther's *Sermon or Instruction on How a Christian Shall Prepare for Death with Joy*.

[Preparing for Death[35]]

Because this letter will go out in print for people to read, I regard it useful to add some brief instructions on how one should care and provide for the soul in the time of death. We have done this orally from the pulpit, and still do so every day in fulfillment of the ministry to which we have been called as pastors.

First, one must admonish the people to attend church and listen to the sermon so that they learn through God's word how to live and how to die. It must be noted that those who are so uncouth and wicked as to despise God's word while they are in good health should be left unattended when they are sick unless they demonstrate their remorse and repentance with great earnestness, tears, and lamentation. Those who want to live like a heathen or a dog and do not publicly repent should not expect us to administer the sacrament to them[36] or have us count them a Christian. Let them die as they have lived because we shall not throw pearls before swine nor give to dogs what is holy [Matt. 7:6]. Sad to say, there are many churlish, hardened ruffians who do not care for their souls when they live or when they die. They simply lie down and die like unthinking hulks.

Second, everyone should prepare in time and get ready for death by going to confession and taking the sacrament once every week or fortnight. They should become reconciled with their neighbor and make their will so that, if the Lord knocks and they depart before a pastor or chaplain can arrive, they have provided for their souls,[37] have left nothing undone, and have committed themselves to God. When many are dying and only two or three pastors are on duty, it is impossible to visit everyone, to give instruction, and to teach each one what a Christian ought to know in the anguish of death. Those who have been careless and negligent in these matters must account for themselves. That is their own fault. After all, we cannot set up a private pulpit and altar daily at their bedsides simply because they have despised the public pulpit and altar to which God has summoned and called them.

Third, if someone wants the chaplain or pastor to come, let the sick send word in time to call him and do so early on, before the illness overwhelms the patient and neither senses nor reason remain. The reason I say this is that some are so negligent that they make no request and send no message until the soul is perched for flight on the tip of the tongue[38] and they are no longer rational or able to speak. Then we are told, "Dear Sir, say the very best you can to him," etc. But earlier, when the illness first began, they wanted no visit from the pastor, but instead would say, "Oh, there's no need. I hope he'll get better." What should a diligent pastor do with such people who neglect both body and soul? They live and die like beasts in the field. They want us to teach them the gospel at the last minute and administer the sacrament to them as they were accustomed to it under the papacy when nobody asked whether they believed or understood the gospel but just stuffed the sacrament down their throats as if into a bread bag.

This won't do. If they cannot talk or indicate by a sign that they believe, understand, and desire the sacrament—particularly if they have willfully neglected it—we will not give it to them just anytime they ask for it. We have been commanded not to offer the holy sacrament to unbelievers but rather to believers who can state and confess their faith. Let the others alone in their unbelief; we are guiltless because we have not been slothful in preaching, teaching, exhortation, consolation, visitation, or in anything else that pertains to our ministry and office.[39] This, in brief, is our instruction and what we practice here. We do not write this for you in Breslau, because Christ is with you and without our aid he will amply instruct you and supply your needs with his own ointment. To him be praise and honor together with God the Father and the Holy Spirit, world without end. Amen.

[On Cemeteries]

Because we have come upon the subject of death, I cannot refrain from saying something about burials. First of all, I leave it to the doctors of medicine and others with greater experience than mine in such matters to decide whether it is dangerous to maintain cemeteries within the city limits. I do not know and do not claim to understand whether vapors and mists arise out of graves to pollute the air. If this were so my previously stated warnings constitute ample reason to locate cemeteries outside the city. As we have learned, all of us have the responsibility of warding off this poison to the best of our ability because God has commanded us to care for the body, to protect and nurse it so that we are not exposed needlessly. In an emergency, however, we must be bold enough to risk our health if that is necessary. Thus we should be ready for both—to live and to die according to God's will. For "none of us lives to himself and none of us dies to himself," as St. Paul says, Rom. 15 [14:7].

It is very well known that the custom in antiquity, both among Jews and pagans, among saints and sinners, was to bury the dead outside the city. Those people were just as prudent as we claim to be ourselves. This is also evident in St. Luke's Gospel, when Christ raised from the dead the widow's son at the gates of Nain (for the text [Luke 7:12] states, "He was being carried out of the city to the grave and a large crowd from the city was with her"). In that country it was the practice to bury the dead outside the town.

Christ's tomb, also, was prepared outside the city. Abraham, too, bought a burial plot in the field of Ephron near the double cave where all the patriarchs wished to be buried. The Latin therefore employs the term *efferi*, that is, "to carry out," by which we mean "carry to the grave." They not only carried the dead out but also burned their bodies to powder to keep the air as pure as possible.

My advice, therefore, is to follow these examples and to bury the dead outside the town.[40] Not only necessity but piety and decency should induce us to provide a public burial ground outside the town, that is, our town of Wittenberg.

A cemetery rightfully ought to be a fine quiet place, removed from all other localities, to which one can go and reverently meditate upon death, the Last Judgment, the resurrection, and say one's prayers. Such a place should properly be a decent, hallowed place, to be entered with trepidation and reverence because doubtlessly some saints rest there. It might even be arranged to have religious pictures and portraits painted on the walls.

But our cemetery, what is it like? Four or five alleys, two or three marketplaces, with the result that no place in the whole town is busier or noisier than the cemetery. People and cattle roam over it at any time, night and day. Each house has a door or pathway to it and all sorts of things take place there, probably even some that are not fit to be mentioned. This totally destroys respect and reverence for the graves, and people think no more about walking across it than if it were a burial ground for executed criminals. Not even the Turk[41] would dishonor the place the way we do. And yet a cemetery should inspire us to devout thoughts, to the contemplation of death and the resurrection, and to respect for the saints who rest there. How can that be done at such a common place through which everyone must walk and into which everyone's door opens? If a cemetery is to have some dignity, I would rather be put to rest in the Elbe[42] or in the forest. If a graveyard were located at a quiet, remote spot where no one could make a path through it, it would be a spiritual, proper, and holy sight and could be so arranged that it would inspire devotion in those who go there. That would be my advice. Follow it, who so wishes. If anyone knows better, let him go ahead. I am no man's master.

[Conclusion]

In closing, we admonish and plead with you in Christ's name to help us with your prayers to God so that we may do battle with word and precept against the real and spiritual pestilence of Satan in his wickedness with which he now poisons and defiles the world—that is, particularly against those who blaspheme the sacrament,[43] though there are other sectarians also. Satan is infuriated and perhaps he feels that the day of Christ is at hand. That is why he raves so fiercely and tries to rob us of the Savior, Jesus Christ. Under the papacy Satan was simply "flesh" so that even a monk's cap had to be regarded as sacred. Now he is nothing more than sheer "spirit," and Christ's flesh and word are no longer supposed to mean anything. They made an answer to my treatise long ago, but I am surprised that it has not yet reached me at Wittenberg.[44] [When it does] I shall, God willing, answer them once again and let the matter drop. I can see that they will only become worse. They are like a bedbug which itself has a foul smell, but the harder you rub to crush it, the more it stinks. I hope that I've written enough in this pamphlet for those who can be saved so that—God be praised—many may thereby be snatched from their jaws and many more may be strengthened and confirmed in the truth. May Christ our Lord and Savior preserve us all in pure faith and fervent love, unspotted and pure until his day. Amen. Pray for me, a poor sinner.

Annotations

1   It is not known when Hess first wrote to Luther, nor when he repeated his request. The plague first hit Breslau in August 1525, yet an extant letter from Luther to Hess on 22 April 1526 makes no mention of the request (WA Br 4:60–61).

2   This translation is based on the original German edition in WA 23:339–79 and the English translation in LW 43:113–38.

3   Luther is referring to his many ongoing health problems. By this time, he had experienced kidney stones, angina, fainting spells, and buzzing in his ear. On 6 July 1527, Luther had severe circulatory problems and thought he was dying. After that incident, he suffered from headaches that left him unable to read or write for a time. He interpreted all of these ailments as God's disciplining of him, though he does not name specific sins.

4   When Luther began writing this response, the plague was rumored to be near Wittenberg. It arrived there on 2 August 1527, which suggests that Luther began writing this open letter shortly before then.

5   Nearly all Christians during the late-medieval and Reformation periods interpreted plagues and other disasters as God's just punishment for sin. See Ronald Rittgers, "Protestants and Plague: The Case of the 1562/63 Pest in Nuremberg," in Franco Mormando and Thomas Worcester, *Piety and Plague: From Byzantium to the Baroque*, Sixteenth Century Essays and Studies 78 (Kirksville, MO: Truman State University Press, 2007).

6   That is, faith in its infancy, and thus only able to drink milk.

7   In other words, those who are strong in faith and willing to accept death cannot expect all Christians to do the same.

8   This is an example of someone who flees death in an unfaithful way.

9   Priests were often criticized for fleeing when the plague arrived, and it seems they regularly fled. Cf. Robert S. Gottfried, *The Black Death: Natural and Human Disaster in Medieval Europe* (New York: Free Press, 1983). The plague hit clergy particularly hard, likely because the Sacrament of Unction, or last rites, forced clergy to be in close proximity to those who were dying

of the disease. The close quarters of monastic communities also made them very susceptible to plague. Cf. Joseph P. Byrne, *Daily Life During the Black Death* (Westport, CT: Greenwood, 2006), 115–30; and William Chester Jordan, *Europe in the High Middle Ages* (London: Penguin Books, 2001), 297.

10   Luther's emphasis on comforting the consciences of the dying diverges from standard late-medieval practice, which urged dying Christians to avoid sin on the deathbed in order to aid in their salvation. See Luther's *Sermon on Preparing for Death*, and Austra Reinis, *Reforming the Art of Dying* (Aldershot, UK: Ashgate, 2007).

11   St. Athanasius (c. 296–373) was a fourth-century bishop of Alexandria best known for his role in formulating the doctrine of Christ as both fully human and fully divine. He was exiled or fled Alexandria numerous times during his tenure there because of opposition to him.

12   According to the book of Acts, a riot broke out in the marketplace in Ephesus because of Paul's preaching against a local goddess. Local officials and Paul's companions both urged Paul not to enter the marketplace.

13   Luther's advice follows the paradigm he set out most famously in *On the Freedom of a Christian*: "A Christian is a perfectly free lord of all, subject to none. A Christian is a

perfectly dutiful servant of all, subject to all" (LW 31:344; *The Annotated Luther* 1:488). Here Luther explicates what this means for the plague: the only law a Christian must follow is the law of love—in this case, caring for the sick, maintaining public services, and tending to spiritual needs.

14   Luther argues against a hierarchy of spirit over flesh. Instead, he sees the instinct toward self-preservation as something given by God and not forbidden unless it interferes with the love of God and neighbor.

15   Matt. 6:25: "Therefore I tell you, do not worry about your life, what you will eat or what you will drink, or about your body, what you will wear. Is not life more than food, and the body more than clothing?"

16   In this paragraph Luther shows the foolishness of pseudo-heroism in the name of faith by sarcastically imagining the extreme practices that this line of reasoning might engender.

17   Those with weak faith are not condemned here but, rather, encouraged to follow their consciences and to submit themselves to God's will amid all dangers.

18   Luther began this section in mid-September after taking a break in his writing. From this point onward, we see Luther responding not only to the question posed by the Breslau

clergy, but also the presence of the plague in Wittenberg at this time (LW 43:125).

19   The German term Luther uses for "neighbor" here is *Nächste*, literally, "whoever is near you."

20   In Luther's catechisms and other explications of the Ten Commandments, he emphasizes that the commandments both prohibit and prescribe. Thus, the commandment not to kill means for him that Christians must offer aid for others' physical needs or they are guilty of murder.

21   In sixteenth-century Europe, hospitals existed only in larger towns, and then only where a private citizen or group endowed and sustained them. Those hospitals that existed were usually staffed by convents or monasteries, so the abolition of monasticism in the Reformation threatened the survival of such hospitals. Later in the sixteenth century, specialized plague hospitals were often established to isolate plague patients and to provide them medical and spiritual care. See Otto Ulbricht, *Die leidige Seuche* (Cologne: Böhlau Verlag, 2004).

22   This theory of how pestilence is communicated reflects the early modern belief, received via Hippocrates and Galen, that infection is spread by foul air. Medieval towns often limited the locations and hours of butchers and leather tanners so that they would not foul the air and thereby spread illness.

23   In sixteenth-century thought, the devil and excretion were closely linked. It was thought that the devil preyed on humans while they were using the toilet because that was where they were most degraded, and thus most vulnerable. Luther once said that he discovered the gospel while on the toilet (WA TR 2:177, 8ff.). Whether literally true or not, it illustrates Luther's belief that Christ's redemption reaches the entire range of human experience. See Heiko A. Oberman, *Luther: Man between God and the Devil*, trans. Eileen Walliser-Schwarzbart (New Haven: Yale University Press, 1989), 154–56.

24   Luther often suggests exact wording to use when fighting the devil and reassuring oneself of God's grace.

25   Here we see that the plague was sometimes interpreted as a punishment of particular people for particular deeds. Likewise, those who did not become ill when they faithfully nursed the sick are understood as receiving immunity because of their faithfulness.

26   Such chastisement was meant for Luther himself as well as the reader. During Luther's spiritual struggles in 1527 and 1528, he often rebuked himself for succumbing to despair, and he charged himself with blasphemy. Cf. WA Br 4:226,8–227,23.

27   Those who did not care for the poor are portrayed as being at Christ's left hand in Matthew 25. To sin "on the left

hand" means to perpetrate a sin of omission, or not doing something that Christians are commanded to do. To sin "on the right hand" is to do something that is forbidden.

28   Suicide was considered an unforgivable sin at this time, and one that merited certain damnation.

29   Instead of seeing intentional exposure to the plague as a sign of great faith, Luther sees it as a great sin because it can kill not only the person inviting the exposure, but also many others.

30   Because sixteenth-century Europeans thought that the plague was caused by foul air, one remedy was to cleanse the air through fumigation.

31   Luther and others assumed that someone who had been infected could transmit the plague even after recovering from it.

32   Numerous rumors of conspiracy circulated in plague-infested areas. In Geneva, authorities condemned some doctors, apothecaries, and plague workers for spreading the plague in order to increase their business. In the later sixteenth century, plagues in some Catholic areas were blamed on Lutherans. Witches and Jews were also frequently accused of spreading plague. See William Naphy, *Plagues, Poisons and Potions: Plague-Spreading Conspiracies in the Western Alps c. 1530–1640* (Manchester: Manchester University Press, 2002).

33   Hangmen learned their trade through an apprenticeship. Those who had completed the apprenticeship and trained others were called "masters" because they had mastered their trade.

34   In the Old Testament, lepers and others with chronic skin diseases were thought to be ritually impure. Leviticus 13:45–46 requires lepers to live alone outside of the community and to identify themselves as unclean. The practice of maintaining lepers' houses, or leprosaria, at the edge of town was revived in Europe in the High Middle Ages.

35   Confession was the central ritual in preparing for death, both in the late-medieval church and in Luther's revision of the practice. In the late-medieval church, confession and absolution obtained forgiveness for sin, and thus improved the individual's chance for salvation. In Luther's reinterpretation, confession and absolution assured the Christian of God's mercy, and thereby offered consolation and assurance of salvation on the deathbed.

36   Communion was normally administered to the dying as part of a Christian death. See Luther's *Sermon on Preparing to Die* for more on practices surrounding death.

37   Confession was the central ritual in preparing for death, both in the late-medieval church and in Luther's revision of the practice. In the late-medieval church, confession and absolution

obtained forgiveness for sin, and thus improved the individual's chance for salvation. In Luther's reinterpretation, confession and absolution assured the Christian of God's mercy, and thereby offered consolation and assurance of salvation on the deathbed.

38   At this time the soul was thought to exit the body via the mouth.

39   In other words, pastors can refuse to administer the sacrament to someone if they have faithfully carried out their office, and thereby exhorted and encouraged their parishioners to receive the sacrament regularly.

40   In the Middle Ages, Christians began to bury the dead in churches and churchyards in order to be near the holy things contained in a church. Beginning in the late fifteenth century, many cities closed their churchyard cemeteries because of overcrowding and the smell exuded by the corpses. Luther alludes to a debate at the time over whether the smell polluted the air and thereby spread disease, but his main concern is that the graveyard be removed so that it may be a peaceful place. See Craig Koslofsky, *The Reformation of the Dead: Death and Ritual in Early Modern Germany, 1450–1700* (New York: St. Martin's, 2000), esp. 40–77.

41   "The Turk" refers to the people of the Ottoman Empire, which had grown enormously over the fifteenth century and

had advanced to the gates of Vienna by the time Luther wrote this work. They were considered a menacing threat to Europe, not least because they were Muslim.

42   The Elbe is the river that flows near Wittenberg.

43   This is a reference to Luther's conflict with fellow reformers Andreas Karlstadt (c. 1480–1541) and Ulrich Zwingli (1484–1531), both of whom emphasized the spiritual presence of Christ in the Lord's Supper and rejected Luther's view that Christ's body and blood were physically present in the elements. Their debate was carried on via a pamphlet war from 1524 to 1529 and escalated to include several more theologians. At the Marburg Colloquy in 1529, Luther and Zwingli met in an effort to agree on Protestant doctrine. Their failure to reach agreement on the issue of Christ's presence in the sacrament split the Protestant movement into two distinct factions.

44   From January to March 1527 Luther wrote *That These Words of Christ, "This Is My Body," etc., Still Stand Firm against the Fanatics* (LW 37:13–150; *The Annotated Luther* 3:163–274). Zwingli's response, *That These Words . . . Will Always Retain Their Ancient, Single Meaning, and Martin Luther with His Latest Book Has by No Means Proved or Established His Own and the Pope's View*, arrived in Wittenberg on 11 November 1527.

Image Credits